# SKETCHES
*followed by*
# TAO POETRY KIT

poems by

Seb Doubinsky

**LEAKY BOOT PRESS**

*Sketches* followed by *Tao Poetry Kit*
by Seb Doubinsky

First published in 2019 by
Leaky Boot Press
http://www.leakyboot.com

Copyright © 2019 Seb Doubinsky
All rights reserved

No part of this book may be reproduced or
transmitted in any form or by any means,
electronic, mechanical, photocopying,
recording, or otherwise, without prior
written permission of the author.

ISBN: 978-1-909849-71-6

# SKETCHES

# Sketches

the moon rests
on the thick cushion
of the night
like a huge pearl
—unattainable treasure

## Seb Doubinsky

transparent staircase
between two buildings
a man walks down
not transparent

## Sketches

this is a simple poem
it doesn't say much
but it is full of images

## Seb Doubinsky

oh, who will sing the impermanence of science,
gods and borders
and rejoice in hearing the simple song
of a child walking down the street?

## SKETCHES

the cat is gone
the house mourns its absence
only the birds sing louder

*(For Molly, sweet cat)*

april is the sweetest month of death
when daily love has to be unlearned
and absence becomes a faithful companion

## SKETCHES

a lone white cloud
drifts by in the distance
Mount Fuji in Denmark

## Seb Doubinsky

inspiration quietly leaves
to smoke a cigarette
the poet doesn't notice
until he feels like smoking too
and cannot find his lighter

## Sketches

the night gets cold
and it snuggles against the city
to keep warm

## Seb Doubinsky

in the middle, the work
no center, no periphery
just a constant vibration
changing shape every second,
expressing the absolute nothingness
of all out thoughts and feelings

## Sketches

two poets meet
how are you
how are you
silence
silence
fine
fine
silence
silence

night falls on the eternal city
cold breeze like a kiss of stone
the lovers keep warm
through their chained hands

## Sketches

the skin is thinner than the heart
it bleeds when scratched
and hurts when chafed
but many stop at the skin
and mistake it for the heart

## Seb Doubinsky

the empty house relaxes
welcoming birds and clouds
for an early morning tea

## Sketches

is freedom a thought or a state?
the grass says nothing
the cat says nothing
the wind says nothing
poetry says nothing

# Seb Doubinsky

the sun takes off its shirt
we sweat and stare in awe
blinded by its muscles

## Sketches

don't kerouac me
don't burroughs me
don't ginsberg me
don't chinaski me
you stupid asshole
just drink your beer
and shut the fuck up

## Seb Doubinsky

the sun waits outside
melting ice-creams and shadows
come in come in
the iced-tea is ready
and I need some company

## Sketches

stillness of the mirror
only the image moves
then disappears

stillness of the image
only the mirror moves
then disappears

## Seb Doubinsky

breathe in
breathe out
like the world

## SKETCHES

poetry is made of
tiny tiny words
that break the wall of sound
forever shattering
the empty blueness
of the sky

# Seb Doubinsky

I sit on a chair
on the lawn
under the sun
under the sky
under everything

I sit on a chair
on the lawn
above everything

# Sketches

see this diamond
shining in my palm?
it's only a tiny word
and a great illusion
some call poetry
and others a lie

## Seb Doubinsky

a flock of birds
a fawn
two foxes
our eyes
lost in the wind

# SKETCHES

oh the heavy heart
like a balloon filled
with water
instead of air

# Seb Doubinsky

rumors of war
a breeze makes the leaves dance on the branch
somewhere high above the moon must be shining

# SKETCHES

a pillow filled
with feathers
no birds

## Seb Doubinsky

early morning moon
a pale coin seen
at the bottom of a fountain

## Sketches

add a flower in a vase
on the table
and the poem
is perfect

# Seb Doubinsky

a little rain
a little poetry
balance of powers

## Sketches

a trigonometry formula inscribed
on a 3700 years old tablet
did Babylonians believe that science
would create a better future too?

## Seb Doubinsky

no dog in this poem
not because I don't like dogs
but simply because there isn't any

## Sketches

poetry is a gamble
always raising your stakes
the secret is not to win
but to lose gracefully

## Seb Doubinsky

two or three things
one missing
one always missing

## Sketches

do not give me what you have
do not give me anything
lend me what you have
but do not ask to have it back
—the mystery of poetry

## Seb Doubinsky

it is always difficult
to write a love poem
for the one you love
because you see
love doesn't care so much
about words, allegories or symbols
love cares only about love
that is unwritten
but lived as love

*(To Mette Sofie, my one and only)*

## Sketches

shorter are the days
longer the nights
death and life are struggling
outside my window
in pure whiteness and shadows

# Seb Doubinsky

we are always discovering
what has been discovered
a thousand times before
yet new eyes create new ruins
and new memories awaken the old
—the evidence of living

## Sketches

no words
no images
no sense
yet something
far away and so close
like breath, steps
or the familiar
knock of death
on the wooden table

## Seb Doubinsky

the cold and the sun
sit outside in the garden
two friends happy to see each other
after a long while

## SKETCHES

a bird flies by
fast shadow
on the frozen ground

# Seb Doubinsky

blueness in the white snowy sky
—hope in minus degrees
or just the indifferent beauty
of nature?

# Sketches

snowflakes
like cherry blossoms
—cold garden

# TAO
## POETRY KIT

# SKETCHES

*"To organize is to destroy."*
Chuang Tzu

# SKETCHES

*wei wu wei*
*wu bu wei*
nothing/everything
in between

## Seb Doubinsky

a king without a crown
is not much of a king
yet much more a king
than a king with a crown

## Sketches

the moon reflected
in my glass of wine
beauty allied
with impatience

SEB DOUBINSKY

small tree
huge lawn
the ant travels slowly

## Sketches

the wise academic who walks
in the university's park
impervious to the butterfly
frolicking around him,
is he really so wise?

## Seb Doubinsky

moving away
is getting closer
like the spring running
from the mountain

## Sketches

ashes blown
by the wind
who knows
where they land?

## Seb Doubinsky

what is the weight of a lightning?
what is the color of air?
let questions fly away
like butterflies in the summer
and drink another glass of wine
while night settles outside
answering everything
including the non-asked

## Sketches

the tao of helping
is also the tao
of letting-go

## Seb Doubinsky

things happen
things don't happen
same things

# Sketches

attention attention attention
we all want attention
yet the blooming flower
does nothing
and gets all of our attention

is a tree slow?
is a tree fast?
does the tree bother?

## Sketches

what is a measure of a measure?
what is the weight of a weight?
what is the meaning of a meaning?
useless questions meaningless thoughts
the tree doesn't think about the sun or the rain

## Seb Doubinsky

the lightning does not think
of perfection
the tree does not think
of strength

be the lightning
or the tree

but do not think
you are like
the lightning
or the tree

## Sketches

tao poetry kit:

a tree
a river
a flute
a pair of sandals
a mountain
the wind
and the distant rumbling
of the city below

www.ingramcontent.com/pod-product-compliance
Lightning Source LLC
LaVergne TN
LVHW041309080426
835510LV00009B/919